FIRST PONY

Kate Needham
Designed by Ian McNee

Illustrated by Mikki Rain
Photographs by Kit Houghton
Consultant: Juliet Mander BHSII

Studio photographs by Howard Allman
Series Editor: Cheryl Evans

Contents

A PONY OF YOUR OWN

All riders dream of a pony of their own, but having a pony is a big commitment. As the owner, you are responsible for looking after your pony, so it's not enough to know how to ride. You need to learn how to care for him too. Here are some questions to ask yourself before you take on that commitment.

Can you really afford to look after him?

It's not just what he costs to buy, you will be paying for everything he needs: food, training, new shoes, vet's fees, tack, rugs, bandages and so on.

Do you have enough time for him?

You can't just take him out for a ride when you feel like it. He needs regular exercise to stay fit, and don't forget about all the chores, such as feeding, grooming or tack cleaning.

Looking after a pony can be great fun but it is hard work and will take up a lot of time. Make sure you know what you are letting yourself in for.

Is there an expert who can help out?

If your parents don't know about ponies, you'll need the support and help of someone who does, such as your instructor or staff at the local stables.

Do you have somewhere to keep him?

A backyard is not big enough. A pony needs at least an acre (½ hectare) of land to graze. You must consider where you might be able to ride him too.

Here are just some of the things you will need to care for your pony.

GETTING EXPERIENCE

The best way to get experience of looking after a pony is to help out at the local stables. By working with several different ponies, you'll learn a lot about how they behave and find out the best ways of dealing with them. When it comes to getting your own pony you'll have a clearer idea of what suits you best. Spending time at the stables is also a good way to meet other horsy people.

Be prepared for hard work and an early start. Pay attention to the daily routine so that you know when to help.

Learn how all the various chores are carried out, such as feeding, mucking out, grooming and tack cleaning.

Watch how the ponies are loaded into a trailer or prepared for the vet or farrier, and pick up tips for when you have to do it.

THE RIGHT PONY FOR YOU

Choose a pony that enjoys the same activities that you do.

A calm pony helps give a nervous rider confidence.

A pony that has already done well will cost more.

Not every pony suits every rider, which is why it's important to assess your own riding ability and confidence before you choose. Think carefully about what you plan to do together, too.

If you are nervous, a pony will sense your fear so look for one with a quiet temperament and gentle manner. An older pony, that has had several young riders, is often calmer than a young one.

If you are confident, you may be able to handle a more fiery pony which will be a greater challenge for your riding. If you are competitive, you might decide to look for a pony that has already done well.

CHOOSING A PONY

Before you choose a pony, think carefully about what you want him for, where you will be able to keep him and how much time you will have to look after him. An experienced person can help you choose what type of pony would suit you best. Here are some of the things you will need to consider.

WHAT TYPE OR BREED?

Many breeds of horses and ponies have been developed over the years. Some of the pony breeds are Welsh, Shetland, POA (Pony of the Americas) Exmoor and Connemara, among others. They vary in temperament, size, looks, strength, and speed. Many ponies are crossbreeds. This means they are a mixture of several breeds.

The boarding arrangement and climate should be taken into account when considering breeds. For example, the Welsh and Shetland breeds are designed to live in the wild and are very hardy.

Your riding interests are an important consideration too. Different breeds excel in different events. For example, Thoroughbreds are known to be fast.

One of the oldest and prettiest breeds is the Arab. But beware of judging a pony by its looks alone! Its temperament and previous training are far more important.

A good first pony will have a quiet, gentle temperament and plenty of experience. A younger, more spirited pony is better for experienced riders.

Thoroughbred

Arab

Exmoor

WHAT HEIGHT?

Choose a pony that is big enough to last you a few years, but not so big that it's too strong for you. Ponies are measured in hands, from the ground to the withers (see page 6). A hand is about 4in (10cm), so a 12½hh pony is 50in (125cm) tall. If you want to compete, check the height limit of classes you want to take part in.

Goldie is an 11½hh, Welsh type palomino, with a stripe.

Legend is a 14hh Connemara dun, with a star.

William is a 13hh, Welsh roan, with a star, a snip and three socks.

4

HOW OLD?

f you don't have much experience it is helpful to have a pony that does. Eight or nine is an ideal age for a first pony. It will have some experience but still have plenty of years ahead of it. You can tell a pony's age by looking at its teeth. A young pony has small straight teeth; an old one has long sloping ones.

At 4 years   At 7 years

A hook appears here.

At 10 years   At 20-25 years

The hook has gone. This groove has started.

COLORS AND MARKINGS

A pony's color and markings are not the most important features, but it is useful to know how they are described.

Grey
white or any shade of grey

Palomino
gold with white mane and tail

Bay
brown with black mane and tail

Chestnut
light brown all over

Skewbald
white and any other color

Brown
dark brown all over

Piebald
patches of white and black

Dun
beige with black mane and tail

Snip   Blaze

Star   Stripe

Sock   Stocking

USEFUL TERMS

- A horse is usually bigger than 14½hh.
- A pony is usually 14½hh or smaller.
- A mare is a female.
- A gelding is a male that has been gelded. This means its testicles have been removed. It can be any age.
- A colt is a young male, that hasn't yet been gelded.
- A filly is a young female.
- A stallion is a male that hasn't been gelded.
- A yearling is one year old.
- A foal is from birth to one year old.

Veeney is a 12½hh New Forest, light grey.

Poem is a 13½hh, black Welsh pony, with a star.

Habibi is a 14hh chestnut Arab, with a blaze and four stockings.

CONFORMATION

Conformation refers to the shape of a pony and the way it is made. Although looks are not the most important thing in an all-around pony, there are some features that affect its performance, health or temperament. The picture below shows the names used for different parts of a pony's body. These are called the "points".

POINTS OF A PONY

Poll

Forelock

Forehead

Muzzle

Chin groove

Throat

Wind pipe

Shoulder

Chest

Forearm

Withers

Girth

Croup

Flank

Hindquarters

Dock

Tail

2nd thigh

Elbow

Sheath

Chestnut

Stifle

Hock

Frog

Bar

Sole

White line

Wall of foot

Knee

Heel

Hoof

Cannon bone

Fetlock

Pastern

FIRST IMPRESSIONS

Take a good overall look at the pony first, from the front, the back and both sides. See if any part of its body seems too large or small. It should fit roughly into a square like this:

Checklist for body
* Back - strong, to carry your weight. A long back is likely to be weak; a short back can be uncomfortable.
* Hindquarters - strong and muscular as this is where all the power comes from.
* Withers - neither too high, as this makes the saddle hard to fit, nor too low, as the saddle may slip. Ideally, about the same height as the croup.
* Chest - wide to allow plenty of room for the heart and lungs.

* Girth - deep to allow space for heart and lungs.
* Neck - slightly arched from the poll to the withers. A "ewe" neck is arched the other way. It may mean a pony is less balanced and therefore harder to control.

Good neck

Ewe neck

THE HEAD

You can tell a lot about a pony's temperament and breeding by its head, in particular its eyes and ears.

The length of neck and size of head are important, as these are what the pony uses to balance with.

A pony showing the whites of his eyes may be nervous or moody. Ears laid back show bad temper.

Large clear eyes are a sign of a kind pony. Ears pricked forward show attentiveness and intelligence.

Loppy ears often indicate an easy-going nature. They might also mean he's not feeling well.

A pony with a "Roman nose" may be related to a heavy carthorse.

A pony with a dish face may have Arab blood in it.

LEGS AND FEET

The legs and feet are extremely important as they take all the shock of a pony's movement. When looked at from in front or behind, both pairs of legs should be straight with the feet pointing forward. If too close, the pony may kick himself. Watch him walk and trot. The movement should be as straight as possible. "Winding" is when a pony puts one foot right in front of the other. "Paddling" is when he swings his legs outward. Both can lead to injuries.

Winding

Paddling

Checklist for legs
* Shoulder - long and sloping back toward the withers for a good stride.
* Elbow - check to see that there is plenty of room between the body for free movement. Try fitting your fist inside.
* Forearm - long and well-muscled for strength.
* Knees - broad and flat.
* Hocks - a clear shape, free of swelling, as these are the hardest working joints.
* Cannon bones - short and straight for strength.
* Fetlocks - free from swelling and heat.
* Pasterns - medium length, ideally sloping at the same angle as the shoulder, as they absorb all the shocks.
* Feet - in good condition with a smooth wall and large frog. Front and back should be matching pairs.

7

BUYING AND TRYING OUT

It's very easy to fall in love with the first pony you see, but always try out several before you decide on the right one for you. It is also essential to get advice from a knowledgeable person, such as your riding instructor. Talk through what type of pony would best suit your level of experience and, if possible, visit the ponies together.

WHERE TO LOOK

The best pony to buy is one you know already. You may have an older friend who has outgrown hers. Ask the instructors at your local stable or pony club whether they know of a suitable pony for sale.

If they don't, ask if they can recommend a breeder. Some breeders have lots of experience matching ponies to children and are very helpful. They may even offer a trial period. Do get a recommendation though, as not all breeders are good.

A horse sale is the worst place to buy from. You can't find out about the pony or ride it, before you buy.

Pony magazines have advertisements of ponies for sale. Look for ponies described as "good first pony", "family pony" or "pony club all-arounder". (See right for some of the abbreviations used.)

Telephone to find out all you can about the pony before you go and visit. Most owners want their ponies to go to a good home, so don't be surprised if they ask you lots of questions too.

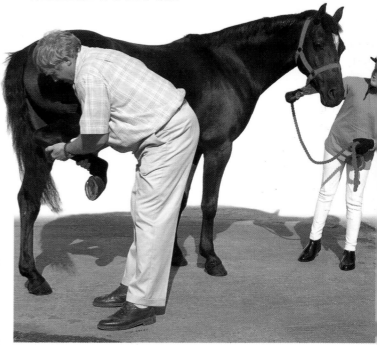

Any pony you buy should be "vetted". This is when a vet does a thorough examination of his body and checks for signs of past illnesses or accidents. This vet is checking the flexibility of the pony's hind leg.

Questions to ask
* How old is he?
* What experience has he?
* How long have you had him?
* Why is he being sold on?
* Does he have any vices (bad habits)? (See opposite).

Questions to answer
* How much experience do you have?
* Where will he be kept?
* What are you hoping to do with him?

Abbreviations
* TB Thoroughbred
* PC Pony Club
* RC Riding Club
* XC Cross country
* SJ Show jumper
* SP Show pony
* HT Hunter trials
* WHP Working hunter pony
* ODE One day event
* PB Part bred
* X Cross bred
* DR Dressage
* LR Leading rein

8

PLANNING YOUR FIRST VISIT

If possible, visit the pony in the field first to check that he is easy to catch. If he is already in the stable, ask to see him turned out later.

See how relaxed he is in the stable. Is he happy or pacing around? Does he like his neighbors? Help groom him to see how he reacts.

Ask to see him led out. Watch from in front, behind and both sides, checking to see that he moves evenly on all four legs. (See page 7.)

Help tack him up. Ask someone else to ride him first, so you can see how he behaves. Ask the rider to take him over a small jump.

Try him out yourself in a confined space, such as an indoor arena. If he seems calm, take him outside to see if he is easily controlled.

See him ridden on the road to make sure he is safe in traffic and to check that he doesn't try to run toward home. (See below.)

Find out if he is good to shoe and load in a trailer. If he is a local pony you could ask the farrier about him yourself.

If you do decide to buy the pony, you must arrange for a vet to examine him. He will check his age, health, and conformation.

VICES TO ASK ABOUT AND AVOID

⁕ Biting equipment or people is a nuisance, and indicates bad temperament.
⁕ Kicking will cause problems with other ponies in a field.
⁕ Bucking may just be high spirits but it can be scary.
⁕ Barn sour describes a pony who always tries to return home. It can become a serious problem.

Never buy a pony that rears. It can be very dangerous and is hard to cure.

⁕ Rearing is a dangerous vice which can be difficult to cure.
⁕ Weaving is when a stabled pony rocks from side to side. It is bad for his legs, and other ponies may copy.
⁕ Cribbing is when a pony grabs the stable door and sucks in air. It can damage his teeth and lungs as well as the stable door.

WHERE WILL HE LIVE?

Most ponies can live out at pasture year-round but ideally you need a stable, too, in case he is ill or gets too fat in the spring. If you don't have a field at home, you will need to lease one nearby or find a boarding stable to keep him at.

KEEPING A PONY AT HOME

It is great to have your own pony at home. It's more convenient, it's easier to keep an eye on him and he will quickly become part of the family. But do make sure that the paddock and stable are suitable (see the checklists below and opposite), and if possible that your pony has a friend. Ponies live naturally in herds and without the company of others they do get lonely.

The main disadvantage for you is that you will have to care for your pony on your own, with little help and advice from experienced people. If you are ill or go away, it may be hard to find someone to look after him for you.

Stable checklist
* At least 3x3½m (10x12ft).
* Built of brick or wood.
* It should have wooden boards halfway up the inside walls.
* The doorway should be about 1½ m (4½ft) wide by 2½m (8ft) tall.
* There must be a top and bottom door which open outward.
* The bottom door should be 1½m (4½ft) high.
* There must be two bolts on the bottom door.

The best companion for him is another pony but a donkey, or even a sheep will do.

Paddock checklist
* At least an acre (½ hectare) of good grass per pony.
* Shelter from bad weather in winter and sun in summer.
* Constant supply of fresh clean water.
* Safe fencing and gates - hedges or post-and-rail are the best type.
* Free from any trash, machinery and poisonous plants, like ragwort or yew.
* Close to home so you can keep an eye on your pony and prevent people feeding dangerous tidbits.

This picture shows you some of the facilities that a good boarding stable might have.

The arena - an enclosed area to exercise in

Nearby bridle paths

Bridle path

A neat muck heap that's easy to get to

KEEPING A PONY BOARDED

A boarding stable is a place where you pay to keep your pony. There are usually several experienced people on hand to help you out, and there is plenty of company for your pony and for you. You can use the stable's facilities and land to ride on too, and you are more likely to meet people to ride with.

You can choose between several different types of stables, depending on how much of the work you plan to do yourself.

Do It Yourself boarding is the cheapest because you do everything yourself. You will need to visit the stable twice each day, before and after school.

Partial board is more flexible, as the stable takes some responsibility for your pony. You still organize his food, muck out his stable and exercise him, but if you go away or can't manage to visit every day, the stable will help out.

Full board is the most expensive, as your pony is completely looked after for you. He will be fed, shod, wormed and even exercised if you want, but find out who will ride him when you are not there.

If you do decide to keep your pony boarded, choose the stable carefully. The checklist below shows a few things to bear in mind when you choose.

A dry hay barn.

Roomy stables, at least 3x3½m (10x12ft) for each pony

A neat tack room

Safe area to groom and tack up in

A trailer to share or rent for shows

Fire extinguisher

Feed room free from rats

Several grass fields

Friendly, helpful people

Boarding checklist
* How close is it to your home? If it is easy to get to, you and your pony will spend more time together.
* Are the stables and fields in good condition?
* Do the ponies already there seem well cared for and happy?
* Is it secure?
* Is there an arena that you can use for exercise? An indoor one is useful on rainy days.
* Are there safe places to ride in the area?
* Are there other children and experienced adults around?
* Who is responsible for the overall running of the stables?

FOOD AND ROUTINE

A pony's natural food is grass. In the wild, ponies wander around eating all the time, so they have small stomachs which are designed to cope with a little food at a time. A pony kept out can survive at pasture alone during the summer, but in winter you need to provide extra food, such as hay.

HAY

Hay, which is dried grass, is the most suitable type of extra food. It should be brownish green and smell sweet. Avoid dusty or moldy hay and, if you buy in bulk, make sure you have somewhere dry to store it.

With several ponies in a field, it is easiest to feed hay loose on the ground, though it can be wasteful. Put down more piles than there are ponies, spaced well apart, so that the fastest eaters don't steal the others' hay. A less wasteful way to feed hay is in a haynet or a hayfeeder.

If you feed hay in a haynet make sure you tie it properly so that your pony can't get his feet caught in it. See how to tie it below.

HOW TO TIE A HAYNET

Ask the farmer before you attach a ring to a tree trunk.

When empty it must not be lower than the pony's chest.

Pull tight before knotting.

Pick a strong fence or sturdy tree in a sheltered spot to tie it to. It needs to be about the height of your pony. Loop the string around the rail or branch.

Thread the string through the mesh at the bottom of the net and pull it up as tight as possible. This will stop the net from sagging as it empties.

Keeping the string pulled tightly upward, tie it back onto itself near the ring. Use a quick-release knot (you can find out how to tie one on page 23).

12

WHAT TO PUT IN AN EXTRA FEEDING

If your pony is working hard, he may need a small feeding for extra energy.

This could be a grain or a rich grass such as alfalfa (opposite), sometimes with an addition of vitamin or mineral supplements. Processed pony food made into pellets (below) is handy, but more expensive.

Most ponies love rich food and gobble it down fast. If you feed a more bulky food, such

as hay, at the same time, it will slow him down and help him to digest.

A carrot or an apple is a good treat, but always cut it into long pieces. If chopped small, it can get stuck in his throat.

It can be dangerous to feed too much, so always get expert advice on quantities.

Rules of feeding
* Feed little and often.
* Feed plenty of roughage, such as grass or hay.
* Feed according to size, age, work and temperament.
* Feed at the same time each day.
* Feed good quality food.
* Feed something succulent every day, such as a carrot.
* Don't work for at least one hour after feeding.
* Don't feed when hot and tired, let him cool down first.
* Make no sudden changes to his diet.
* Keep feed bowls clean.

PLANNING A DAILY ROUTINE

Ponies are creatures of habit and are much happier with a regular routine. It's as if they have a built-in clock. They can get very upset if things don't happen at the usual time.

Try to organize it so that you do each task in the same order and at the same time every day. The list opposite is a good routine to follow if caring for a pony while at school.

Before school
* Catch your pony and check that he is warm and well (see page 30).
* Check his water. In winter you may need to break the ice if it has frozen over.
* Feed him his grain. If stabled, turn out to grass.
* Pick up droppings from field and muck out stable.

After school
* Catch your pony and give him a quick grooming.
* Tack him up and take him out for exercise.
* Let him cool down and brush off any dry sweat. Then turn him out.
* If stabled at night, groom him thoroughly, straighten his bedding and give him water, feed and hay.

Ponies get used to things happening at the same time each day and hate to be kept waiting - especially for food.

13

VETS AND FARRIERS

Every pony owner needs a good vet to give vaccinations, advise about worming doses, check teeth and be on hand when a pony is sick. A farrier is the person who looks after a pony's feet and shoes, and is equally important. Ask around to find out who is best locally.

WHEN TO GET YOUR PONY RESHOD

A pony needs regular visits to (or from) a farrier to have his feet trimmed. If he is ridden on the roads, he will need shoes to protect his feet and the shoes need to be replaced about once every six weeks. Have your pony ready for the farrier with cleanly picked out feet. See below.

Signs he needs shoeing
* The clinches are risen. These are the ends of the nails that hold the shoe on.
* A shoe is loose. You will hear it "clank" on the road.
* He's lost a shoe.
* Part of the shoe has worn thin.
* The foot has grown too long.

Your farrier is an important friend so make your pony behave while he's at work.

LIFTING UP AND PICKING OUT THE FEET

Have the hoofpick ready in the other hand.

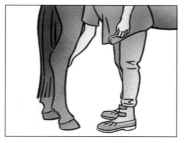

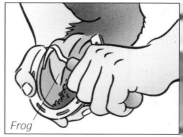

Frog

For the front leg, run your hand down the back of the pony's leg. You may need to lean against him to make him lift his foot.

For the back leg, run your hand down the front of the hock. Grasp the toe as he picks up his foot, so your arm is in front of his leg.

Gently pick out any mud from the foot. Always start from the top, by the heel and move down either side of the frog, toward the toe.

VACCINATIONS

Your pony needs to be vaccinated against equine encephalomyetis and tetanus. Both illnesses are easy to prevent but hard to cure. He will need an initial course of injections and then a booster every year.

* You will also need to produce a Coggins test certificate for most shows and arenas. This states that the horse is free of Equine Infectious Anemia.

* Tetanus is easily caught from cuts. It can be deadly so it's vital to keep the vaccination up to date.

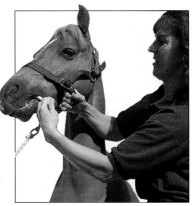

Vaccinations are injected into the pony's neck or hindquarters.

TEETH

Your pony needs to go to the dentist as often as you do, which is once every six months. His teeth are growing all the time and may get sharp edges which make his mouth sore.
A horse dentist or vet smooths these edges down by rasping his teeth.
He will also check for wolf teeth. These are small teeth that often cause pain as they grow and may need to be removed.

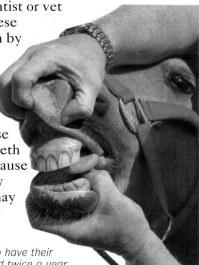

Ponies need to have their teeth inspected twice a year.

WORMING DOSES

All ponies get small types of worms living inside them. A few won't harm them but too many can make them very ill. To stop this from happening you must "worm" your pony. This means feeding him a special worming powder which you can buy from your vet. Ask for advice on a worming program. It usually needs to be done once every 6-8 weeks. See below for more tips about preventing worms.

Keeping worms at bay
* Remove droppings daily from the field. This is where worms live.
* Swap paddocks for a while.
* If possible, let cows or sheep graze in the field. Worms cannot live in their stomachs.
* Dose all ponies that share a field at the same time.

IDENTIFICATION

Unfortunately, ponies do get stolen and it can be hard to get them back. A good prevention is by an identifying number on the pony. Until recently this was done by branding. Now microchips that can be read by a scanner are inserted under a pony's skin . Don't worry - it shouldn't hurt him.

CHOOSING TACK

When you buy a pony you may well get his saddle and bridle thrown in, especially if his old rider has outgrown them. This is often useful, as second-hand tack is usually more comfortable than new, as long as it is in good condition. The leather should be supple and the stitching secure. Even if your tack is passed on, you must make sure that it fits well.

THE SADDLE

The saddle distributes your weight evenly over your pony's back. It can also help you to sit correctly. Saddles are expensive but if taken care of properly they last a lifetime, so buy the best you can afford.

Never buy a cheap one. Poor quality leather can make your pony sore and, if it breaks, puts you in danger. A good quality second-hand one is a much better buy.

There are different types of saddles for jumping or dressage, but for all-around use, choose a general-purpose saddle. It must be the right length and width, so have your pony's back measured by an expert.

Cantle

Seat

The tree, which is made of wood, is the framework of the saddle.

Pommel

Stirrup guard

Knee roll adds comfort for the rider.

Panel

Buckle guards stop girth buckles from wearing away the saddle flap.

The gullet keeps any weight off the spine.

Girth straps

Checklist for saddle fit

* It should lie flat on the pony's back, with the weight evenly distributed.
* It must not be too long, or it will press on the loins.
* You should be able to see daylight when you look down the spine from the pommel or the cantle.

* The pommel must not press on the withers - make sure that you can fit four fingers comfortably between them.
* It should not slip when the pony moves.
* The panels should be evenly stuffed - check by looking from behind.

* If buying second-hand, check that the tree is not broken. With the pommel

in one hand and the cantle against your side, pull toward you. All saddles will give a little but if the tree is broken it will start to fold. Ask for an expert's opinion.

WHICH GIRTH?

The girth is the only thing holding the saddle on, so make sure you get a safe and comfortable one. They come in different lengths so measure your pony before you buy.

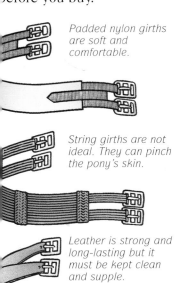

Padded nylon girths are soft and comfortable.

String girths are not ideal. They can pinch the pony's skin.

Leather is strong and long-lasting but it must be kept clean and supple.

WHAT SIZE STIRRUP?

The wrong size stirrup can be dangerous. If you fall you want your foot to slip out of the stirrup easily. If too small, your foot may get wedged into it; if too big, it may slide all the way through.

Wear your riding boots when you go to fit your stirrup. There should be about 1cm (½in) on either side of your boot.

You will need to buy stirrup leathers separately. Buy them long enough to allow for adjustment, but not so long that they trail off the saddle.

New ones are likely to stretch as you use them and the one you use to mount may end up longer. To stop this from happening, switch them around from time to time.

1cm (½in)

You can add rubber treads which help to stop your foot from slipping through.

Rubber stirrup tread

Safety stirrups have a rubber band at the side which flicks open if your foot is pulled out of the stirrup.

PUTTING ON A SADDLE

With the stirrups run up and the girth over the seat, lift the saddle over the withers. Slide it back into position. Never move it forward against the grain of the pony's coat.

Ducking underneath the pony's neck, go around to the other side. Lift the girth down gently. Check underneath the saddle flap to see that the girth straps and guards are lying flat.

Go back around. Check under the flap on this side, then reach underneath for the girth. Fasten it so that it is firm but not tight. You will need to tighten it once you are ready to set off.

THE BRIDLE

Bridles are sold in three different sizes, pony, cob and full, and they come in various widths. Choose one that suits your pony's head.

Most come with a cavesson noseband, which is the mildest. A drop noseband or flash can be useful on a strong pony (see page 26).

Plain leather reins are the most common. If you find them slippery in wet weather, try rubber or braided ones which have a better grip.

Rubber

Plain leather

Braided

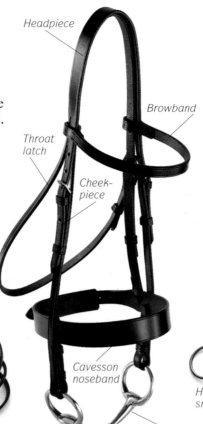

Headpiece

Browband

Throat latch

Cheek-piece

Cavesson noseband

Eggbutt jointed snaffle

The bit is always sold separately. There are hundreds to choose from but the best type for a first pony is a snaffle, which is the mildest. An eggbut jointed snaffle is a good choice. It has smooth rings that prevent the bit pinching the corners of the pony's mouth. Stronger bits can be helpful but they can also do lots of harm, so ask your instructor for advice before trying one out.

If buying a secondhand bridle, undo all the buckles and check for cracks in the leather.

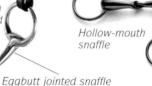

Loose ring snaffle

Hollow-mouth snaffle

Double-jointed snaffle

PUTTING ON A SNAFFLE BRIDLE

First make sure that the throat latch and noseband are undone. Untie the lead rope in case he pulls back, and slip the reins over his head. Undo the halter and refasten it around the pony's neck.

Hold the top of the bridle in your right hand. Have the bit on your left hand with your fingers flat. Place your thumb on the bar of his mouth (near the corner where there are no teeth) and squeeze it gently.

As he opens his mouth, slip the bit inside. Then pull the headpiece gently over his ears. Pull his forelock from under the browband. Buckle the throat latch and noseband and check the fit of the bridle. (See opposite.)

Checklist for bridle fit

The throat latch must be loose enough to allow the pony to breath easily. When it is fastened, you should be able to fit your fist inside it.

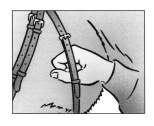

The cavesson noseband should sit four fingers below the cheekbones, and be loose enough for you to get two fingers between it and the pony's nose.

The bit reaches the corners of the pony's lips so that they are just wrinkled and it looks as though he's smiling. It should stick out about 5mm (¼in) on each side.

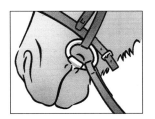

The browband sits just below the ears, but not touching them. It should fit closely, but not so tightly that it pulls the bridle forward over the pony's head.

THE HALTER

A halter is what you use for catching and leading your pony. It can be either leather or nylon. You need a lead rope with a snap to fasten onto the back of it.

Like bridles, halters are sold in three sizes. Once fitted, it must be loose enough for the pony to chew easily but tight enough to stop him from putting a foot through it.

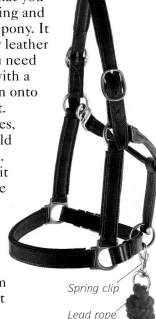

Spring clip

Lead rope

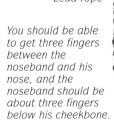

You should be able to get three fingers between the noseband and his nose, and the noseband should be about three fingers below his cheekbone.

OTHER THINGS YOU WILL NEED

For grooming and tack cleaning	For feeding	For mucking out
Dandy brush Body brush Hoof pick Metal and rubber curry combs Sponges Hoof oil and brush Saddle soap Oil for tack	Mouse-proof feed cans Buckets Feed bowls	Fork Broom Shovel Wheelbarrow

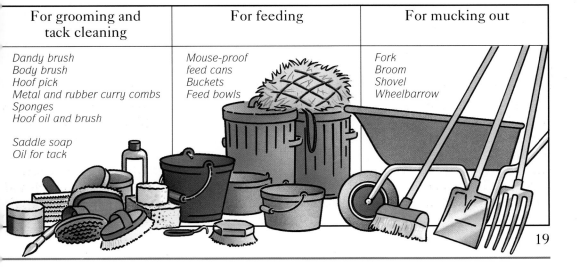

SETTLING IN

It will take a little while for a new pony to fit in and feel comfortable with his surroundings. Don't be tempted to show him off to all your friends on the first day. He will be much happier left alone to get used to his new home quietly. Handle him gently so as not to frighten him, but firmly so that he knows who is boss.

THE FIRST DAY AT HOME

Plan your pony's first day at his new home carefully. If he is to live outside, bring him home early so that he has plenty of daylight hours to get used to his new field and companions.

In all herds of ponies there is a pecking order, where one pony is boss, another number two, and so on. If your pony is to live with a lot of others, see if it is possible to turn him out with just a couple of the quieter ones to start with. Avoid turning a new pony out at feeding time, as this is when the others will be most aggressive.

Don't worry if your pony is left on his own at first. After a few weeks, his position in the pecking order will be established and he will have his own special friends.

If you do bring your pony home at night, settle him in a clean stable, and turn him out the next day.

When two ponies first meet they usually sniff noses, stomp and squeal.

TURNING YOUR PONY OUT

Wait until the other ponies are far away from the gate, then open it wide so that it doesn't swing and catch your pony's legs. Lead your pony through it.

Turn your pony to face the gate and close it. Remove his halter and step out of the way. Push him away from you as you turn, so he doesn't step on your toes.

When turning several ponies out together, let them all loose at the same time. Otherwise one person will be left struggling as the others gallop off.

APPROACHING AND CATCHING YOUR PONY

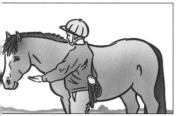

Walk quietly toward him talking calmly as you go. Never come up from behind as your pony will not see you and may be surprised and frightened.

Keeping the halter behind you so he can't see it, approach his shoulder. Pat him as soon as you are near. You could take a few pellets as a reward.

Poll

Place the lead rope over his neck and slip the noseband over his nose. Lift the headpiece over his poll and fasten. For tips on catching difficult ponies see page 25.

LEADING YOUR PONY

Wear a hard hat and gloves.

Always lead from the left, unless on the road when you lead from the right. Have one hand near the halter and the other near the end of the rope.

Stand by his shoulder and say "walk on". He should move forward with you. Never pull him. Push gently forward if he is reluctant to move.

When turning, push him away from you. He will stay better balanced and avoid treading on your toes. For longer distances, use a chain on for better control.

21

BECOMING FRIENDS

A pony soon recognizes the person who visits each day and feeds him, but the more time you spend together, out riding or in the stable yard, the better you will grow to understand each other.

YOUR PONY'S SENSES

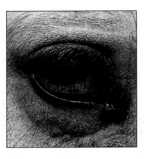

Large eyes are a sign of a kind pony. If frightened, they may look white.

The five senses are sight, taste, hearing, touch and smell. With eyes on each side of his head, your pony's sight is good. The only place he can't see is behind and immediately in front. He sees things farther in front well, using both eyes.

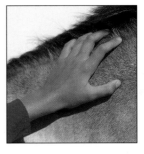

Stroking and patting are soothing gestures that tell your pony he's done well.

You communicate with your pony by touch too. Out riding, your legs tell him what to do. Your pony uses his soft muzzle and long whiskers to touch and investigate things. He greets a friend by touching noses.

If you talk to your pony all the time, he will soon recognize your voice.

His hearing is good too. By moving his ears around, he can sense where a noise is coming from. Although he doesn't really understand what you say, he does understand the tone of your voice. So, if you are mad, sound it. If pleased, pat him as you talk.

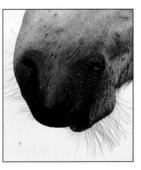

Ponies recognize each other and their home territory by smell.

This also allows him to smell his friends which is how ponies recognize each other. They use their strong sense of smell to check their food too. A crafty pony can gobble up a mixed feed and leave behind the part he dislikes, such as worming powder.

RECOGNIZING BODY LANGUAGE

As you get to know your pony you will sense his moods. He will soon get to sense yours too. You can tell a lot by looking at his eyes and his ears (see page 7). Here are a few more signs that you could look for.

Signs of mood
⬤ Swishing tail or stomping feet mean he's irritated (or maybe it's the flies!)
⬤ Snorting shows he is frightened or spooked.
⬤ Tail clamped down hard can be a sign that he is about to kick. He could also be cold.
⬤ Tail held high shows he is excited about something.

GROOMING

Grooming is essential to keep your pony clean, but it is also one of the best ways to form a bond with your pony. Choose a nice shady place where you can both be comfortable as you work. Tie up with a quick-release knot (see below).

Don't groom a pony that lives outside too much, especially in winter. He needs the natural oils in his coat to keep warm. Just use the dandy brush to get off the mud and give him a good scratch. In the summer you can use the body brush to get a shine on his coat.

In the wild, ponies groom each other, so your pony will appreciate you scratching the parts he cannot reach.

TYING SAFELY WITH A QUICK-RELEASE KNOT

Always tie your pony in an enclosed place, so that if he does pull free he can't escape. Never tie him directly to the ring. Attach a small loop of string to the ring, and fasten the lead rope to this. If he panics and pulls back, the string will break. Make sure that the wall or rail is sturdy and won't give way before the string does. Use a quick-release knot when tying your pony, so that you can untie your pony fast in an emergency. Here's how to tie one:

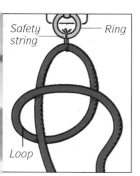

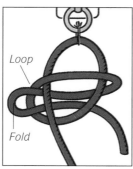

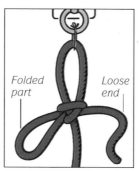

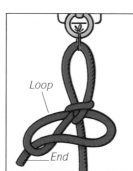

Pull the lead rope through the safety string and make a loop with the end of it across the rest, as shown above.

Fold the remaining rope, take it behind the part that is attached to the pony and pull it through the loop.

Pull down on the folded part, making sure the end doesn't pull through. To undo quickly, pull on the loose end.

If your pony can free himself, thread the end through the loop. Unthread it before pulling for a quick release.

NAUGHTY PONIES

A pony that misbehaves could be frightened or in pain, or he may just be testing you to see what he can get away with. Any bad habit needs to be cured as soon as possible. Never be embarrassed to ask for help. You need to check that you are not doing something wrong before you blame your pony.

WHY PROBLEMS HAPPEN

Cause	Reason	Action
Is he in pain?	Sore back or sharp teeth.	Get the vet to examine him.
	Saddle or bridle do not fit properly.	Ask a professional saddler to check his tack.
	You may be hurting him.	Ask your instructor for advice.
Is he frightened?	Something has made him panic.	Find out what he is scared of and get him used to it quietly.
	You're asking him to face something new.	Let him follow another pony.
	He's had a bad experience in the past.	Use patience to calm his fears and win his trust.
Is he too full of beans?	Too much rich food.	Cut down on high energy foods such as grain or alfalfa hay.
	Not enough exercise.	Ride him more often or turn him out for longer so he gets more exercise.

MAKE SURE HE KNOWS WHO IS BOSS

Some ponies misbehave simply because they know they can get away with it. This is why it is vital to show him that you are in charge right from the start. Ponies are used to a pecking order (see page 20) and you become part of it, so make sure you are at the top not the bottom. Always be strict about stable manners. If you are not boss on the ground, you will stand little chance of being boss out riding.

If you once let your pony think he is boss, he may start to make fun of you and misbehave.

HARD TO CATCH

If a pony is hard to catch, use patience and stealth to teach him to come to you.

Catching tips
* You could leave a halter on, but make sure it is a leather one that fits well (see page 19).
* Take a carrot or handful of grain or pellets. Rattling a bucket is effective, but if he shares a field, watch out for a stampede!

* Get as close as he will allow, hold out your hand with his treat, and make him walk the last few steps, even if it takes ages.
* Ponies hate leaving their friends, so catch him when the others are coming in.
* Bring him in at the same time each day and make him look forward to it by giving him some hay.

TROUBLE MOUNTING

If your pony starts jumping around as you try to get on, make sure he is not in pain. If he is just acting up, try these solutions.

Ask someone to hold him while you mount or put him near a fence so he can't walk forward.

If he is too tall, use a mounting block or find someone to give you a leg up, as shown here.

If he turns to nip you, keep the reins tight and have the one on the other side slightly shorter.

If the saddle slips when you get on, ask someone to hold the stirrup on the other side.

ALWAYS EATING

If you let your pony eat with his bridle on, he may pick up the irritating habit of snatching at every blade of juicy grass while out riding. To stop him from doing this, you need to spot the grass first, hold the reins firmly and kick him on. If it becomes a real problem, you might consider using grass reins.

Grass reins help teach your pony not to eat with a bridle on, but you can't wear them in shows.

Grass reins go from the bit to the "D" rings. They prevent him from putting his head down to eat.

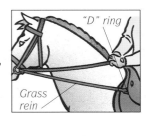

"D" ring

Grass rein

BOLTING

A pony's natural reaction to fear is to run. It is very scary when a pony bolts, but you must try to stay calm. Screaming for help will frighten him even more. Sit tight, with plenty of weight in the saddle and talk calmly to him. Turning large circles may help to slow him down. Have him checked by the vet and if the problem continues ask your instructor to help.

TOO STRONG

Some small ponies are very strong, and if they start to pull against you, can be hard to control. If yours does this, first make sure that he is not in pain from sharp teeth or mouth ulcers. Check his food. Is it too rich? Does he get enough exercise? If he is just playing up, there are various pieces of tack that make a strong pony easier to control (see below), but always ask an expert for advice.

SADDLE SLIPS

If the saddle slips forward check that it fits properly (see page 16). It may be the shape of your pony that is a problem, particularly if he is fat. Try fitting a crupper - a leather strap with a loop that goes around the tail. It fastens to a ring on the back of the saddle (see below).

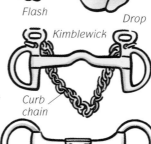

Flash   *Drop*

Kimblewick

Curb chain

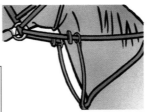

Dr Bristol

Stronger tack
* A flash or drop noseband fastens beneath the bit. It stops the pony from opening his mouth wide and pulling against you.

* A change of bit can help, but the wrong one may make things worse so get advice. The strongest have curb chains that fasten under the chin.

* A running martingale stops the pony from bringing his head up high, where it is difficult to control. It must be fitted carefully.

Some ponies blow out their tummies as you fasten the girth, so check it before you get on and after a few minutes' riding.

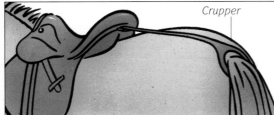

Crupper

If your pony pulls you around while you are leading him, put on a bridle. It will give you more control.

BUCKING

The infrequent buck is not a serious problem. It often just shows that a pony is in high spirits. Check on his routine. You may need to cut back his feed or ride him more frequently.

If he bucks persistently, there may be something wrong that is causing him pain. Ask the vet to look at his back and teeth, and get an expert to check that his tack fits correctly.

If he is simply taking advantage of you, you need patience and forceful riding to straighten him out. Don't stop when he does it. Sit up, keep your leg on him and ride him through it.

SHYING

Shying is when your pony is spooked by something and won't go past it calmly. It can be dangerous when riding on the road. A pony in high spirits is more likely to shy at things so check on his food.

Tips to calm him
* Ride him in an enclosed area before taking him outside.
* Find out what spooks him and try to get him used to it.
* When passing a spooky object, look at it yourself but turn your pony's head away.
* Use your outside leg to stop him from swinging out and ride strongly forward.
* Ride out with a quiet pony to give him confidence.
* Get his eyesight and hearing checked.

BARN SOUR

A pony is barn sour when he refuses to leave his friends. He may stop dead, or he may turn and dash for home. Keep him moving forward. Use a whip if necessary, and carry it on the side he usually turns to. When out riding, try to take a circular route as returning home along the same road can encourage him to turn for home when he feels like it. If he is strong and willful ask an older person to help you.

Acting barn sour leads to rearing, so never let him get away with it.

WHERE TO RIDE

Once you have your own pony, it's up to you to make sure that he gets enough exercise. Otherwise, he may become too lively and hard to handle. It is safest at first, to ride him in an enclosed area such as an indoor or outdoor arena, but once you are used to each other it is fun to explore your local area.

BRIDLE PATHS AND TRAIL RIDING

Trail riding can be a lot of fun for you and your pony but you must make sure that you have permission to cross someone else's land.

Many state and federal parks have trails for riding, but you might need to get permission to ride there as well. Ask at your local stable or park.

Go with someone who knows the area and can show you the route the first few times.

Trail etiquette
* Always keep to the trail, especially when crossing a field planted with crops.
* Be considerate to other users, for example, walk past them, never canter.

* Never ride through the middle of livestock, such as cows or sheep. Go around.
* If the land is very wet, keep off. Riding through will cut it up and make it worse when it dries out.
* Close any gate you open to pass through.
* Be extra careful during harvest time when there is "spooky" machinery.

Riding with friends is nicer for you and for your pony. It's also a lot safer.

Until you get used to your pony, ride out with an experienced person.

SAFETY ON THE ROAD

Riding on the road is not ideal but it is often the only way to reach safer riding areas. Here are some points to remember.

Safety checklist
* Make sure your pony is familiar with traffic before taking him out on the road.
* Have a safe horse on your outside the first time.
* Always keep to the right.
* Where possible, keep to the grass shoulder.
* Try to avoid the busiest periods.
* Thank motorists who slow down. Nod and smile if you can't take your hands from the reins.
* Make sure you know your Highway Code.
* Wear reflective clothing so that you are easily seen.
* Wait for a clear road before passing scary objects.
* If leading a pony on the road, put yourself between the pony and the traffic.
* Your local pony club or 4-H club will have more safety tips.

Raise your hand to thank motorists.

WHAT TO WEAR

You will probably have your own riding gear from the first day you began to ride, but here's a reminder of what you should wear.

Hard hat
Silk

A hard hat that fits well with a chin strap. Make sure it meets current safety standards.

Body protectors are a good safety measure for all types of riding.

Jodhpurs protect your legs from rubbing against the saddle.

Gloves with a good grip protect your hands and keep them warm in cold weather.

Riding boots with a small heel. Tennis shoes or rubber boots can get stuck in the stirrups.

GOING FURTHER

With your own pony there is no limit to how much riding you can do.

One of the best ways to get involved in lots of different events is to join a local pony club or 4-H club. (You can get the address from the organizations listed on page 32).

Joining a local club is a good way to meet fellow riders too.

Pony Club events
* Picnic rides
* Gymkhanas
* Summer camps
* Shows
* Hunter trials
* Stable management courses
* Riding and road safety exams
* Mounted games

CHECKING HIS HEALTH

Your pony can't tell you when he is feeling ill, so it is important to recognize the signs. The main thing is to get to know him well, including all his favorite habits, so that you notice any unusual behavior. Make sure you check him over carefully at least once each day.

SIGNS OF GOOD AND BAD HEALTH

	Head	Ears	Eyes	Nostrils	Coat
Good sign	Looking up Watching your approach	Pricked up Feel warm	Bright and shiny Salmon pink membrane	Pink and clean	Lying flat Looking glossy
Bad sign	Hung low Barely notices your approach	Drooping or laid back Feel cold	Dull Sad-looking	Full of discharge	Dull and patchy Standing on end
	Skin	Ribs	Appetite	Droppings	Legs
Good sign	Loose and supple	Can't be seen Can be felt	Eating up Chewing well	Soft balls that break as they hit the ground Passed about 8 times a day	Check that he is standing square (Resting a back leg is usual but a front one is odd)
Bad sign	Tight and dry Sore or rubbed patches	If you can see them he's too thin If you can't feel them he's too fat	Refusing food Having trouble chewing	Sloppy like a cow's Not passing any at all	Lame or limping Cuts and grazes Heat or swellings

PULSE

Feel for the pulse under the jaw, or just above his eye, here.

A pony's pulse rate should be 36 to 42 beats a minute, at rest. Use two fingers to feel it under his jaw or just above his eye. You may need help finding it at first.

RESPIRATION

Flank

Respiration is his breathing rate. At rest, it should be 8-12 regular breaths a minute. To count them, watch his flanks go in and out or put your hand near his nose.

TEMPERATURE

A pony's temperature should be 38°C (100.5°F). It is taken by putting the thermometer in his bottom and should only be done by an experienced person.

WHEN TO CALL THE VET

If in doubt, call the vet out, but try not to do it outside business hours unless it's an emergency. Consult an experienced person first if there is one around, but if not, call the vet right away. An early visit could stop a serious problem from developing.

Signs to worry about
* Sudden lameness that has no obvious cause. Check for stones in his foot first and consult the farrier if he is around.
* A deep wound that won't stop bleeding and may need stitches.
* Any hot, painful swelling on the legs.
* Continual coughing.

* A pony who won't eat for more than a day.
* Hot feet and a reluctance to move are signs of laminitis which must be dealt with immediately.
* A pony looking at his flanks and kicking his belly may have colic (tummy ache) which is serious, so call the vet immediately.
* Soft or sloppy droppings, or none at all, can also be a sign of colic.

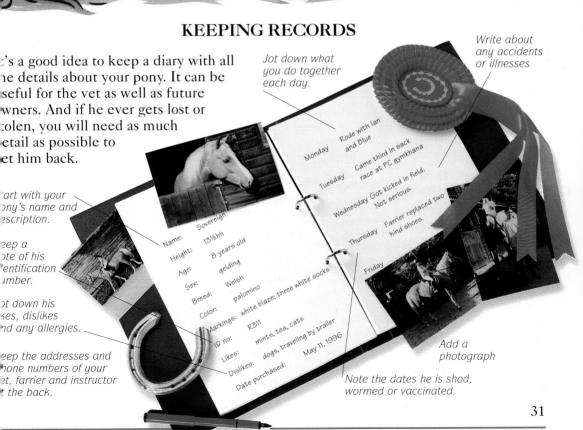

Ponies love to roll for fun and to scratch their own coat. But a pony that keeps rolling, breaks into a sweat and starts kicking his stomach, may be very ill, so call the vet.

KEEPING RECORDS

It's a good idea to keep a diary with all the details about your pony. It can be useful for the vet as well as future owners. And if he ever gets lost or stolen, you will need as much detail as possible to get him back.

Start with your pony's name and description.

Keep a note of his identification number.

Jot down his likes, dislikes and any allergies.

Keep the addresses and phone numbers of your vet, farrier and instructor at the back.

Jot down what you do together each day.

Write about any accidents or illnesses

Monday   Rode with Ian and Blue
Tuesday   Came third in sack race at PC gymkhana
Wednesday Got kicked in field. Not serious.
Thursday Farrier replaced two hind shoes.
Friday

Name: Sovereign
Height: 13½hh
Age: 8 years old
Sex: gelding
Breed: Welsh
Color: palomino
Markings: white blaze; three white socks
ID no: R311
Likes: mints, tea, cats
Dislikes: dogs, traveling by trailer
Date purchased: May 11, 1996

Add a photograph

Note the dates he is shod, wormed or vaccinated.

INDEX

USEFUL ADDRESSES

These organizations can put you in touch with the clubs and events in your country.

American Horse Show Association Inc.
220 East 42nd St, Suite 409
New York NY 10017,
USA.

Canadian Equestrian Federation
1600 James Naismith Drive, Gloucester,
Ontario, K1B 5N4,
Canada.

The British Equestrian Centre
Stoneleigh, Kenilworth
Warwickshire, CV8 2LR
England
(**The Pony Club** is also at this address)

Equestrian Federation of Australia Inc.
52 Kensington Rd,
Rose Park,
S. Australia, 5067

New Zealand Equestrian Federation
P.O. Box 47,
Hastings, Hawke's Bay,
New Zealand.

With thanks to Chloe Albert, Glenn Whitbread, Keely Martin, Nayla Ammar, Stephanie Sarno, all the staff and ponies at Trent Park Equestrian Centre, and Coleman Croft Master Saddlers.